Tim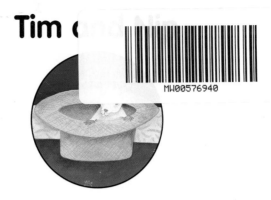

ISBN 10: 0-15-367222-6   ISBN 13: 978-0-15-367222-4

1 2 3 4 5 6 7 8 9 10 179 10 09 08 07

Tim and Nip

by **Lisa deMauro**

Illustrated by **Ande Cook**

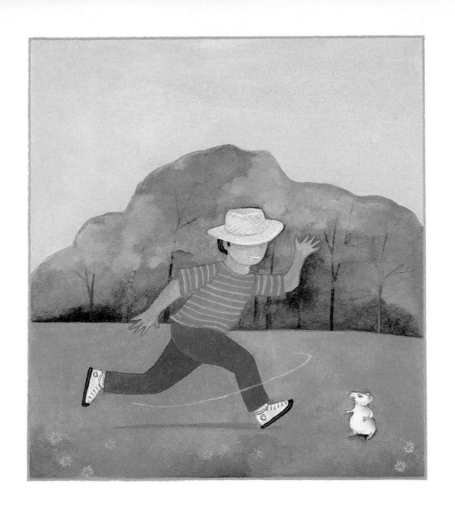

This is Tim.

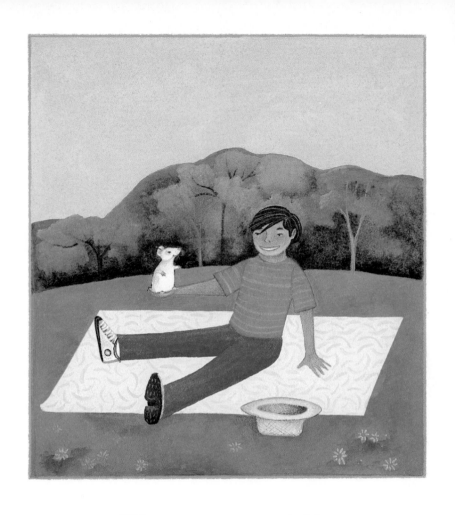

Tim can sit.

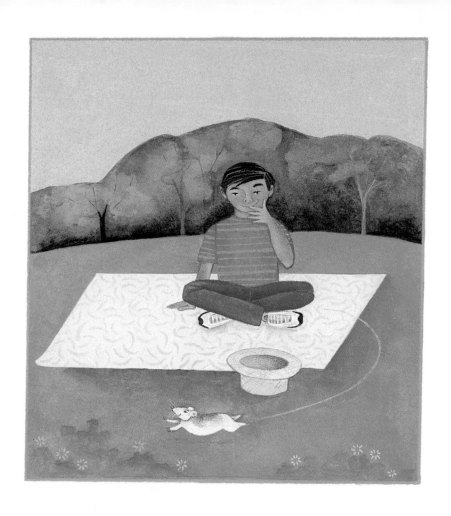

This is Nip.

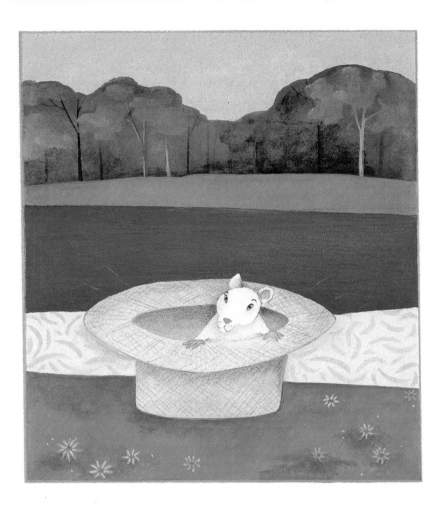

Nip can sit.

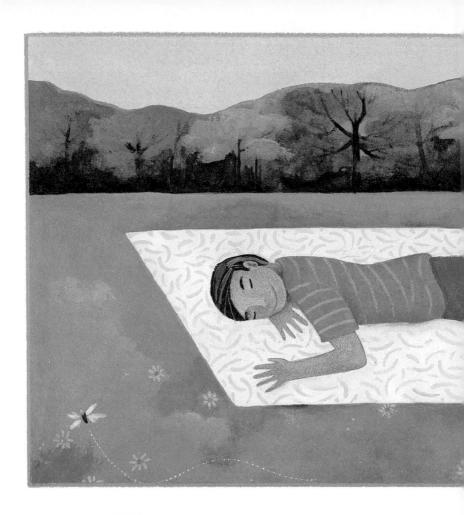

Tim can nap.

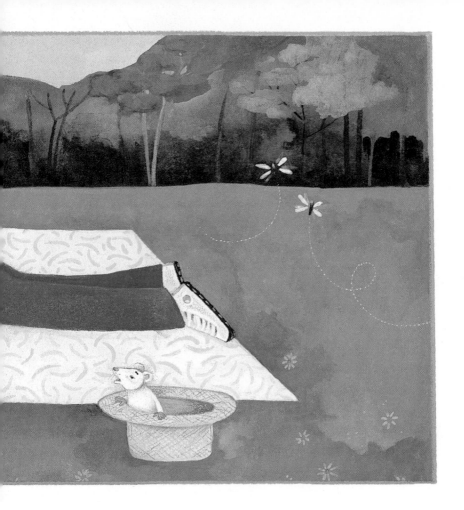

Can Nip nap?

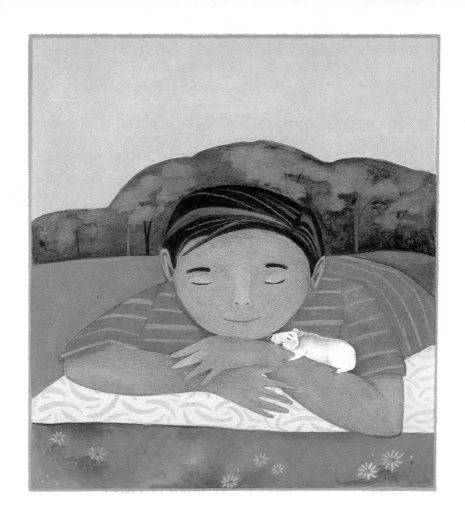

Nip can nap like Tim.

8